NORTH AMERICAN ANIMALS

Northern Cardinals

by Megan Borgert-Spaniol

BELLWETHER MEDIA · MINNEAPOLIS, MN

Note to Librarians, Teachers, and Parents:

Blastoff! Readers are carefully developed by literacy experts and combine standards-based content with developmentally appropriate text.

Level 1 provides the most support through repetition of high-frequency words, light text, predictable sentence patterns, and strong visual support.

Level 2 offers early readers a bit more challenge through varied simple sentences, increased text load, and less repetition of high-frequency words.

Level 3 advances early-fluent readers toward fluency through increased text and concept load, less reliance on visuals, longer sentences, and more literary language.

Level 4 builds reading stamina by providing more text per page, increased use of punctuation, greater variation in sentence patterns, and increasingly challenging vocabulary.

Level 5 encourages children to move from "learning to read" to "reading to learn" by providing even more text, varied writing styles, and less familiar topics.

Whichever book is right for your reader, Blastoff! Readers are the perfect books to build confidence and encourage a love of reading that will last a lifetime!

This edition first published in 2018 by Bellwether Media, Inc.

No part of this publication may be reproduced in whole or in part without written permission of the publisher. For information regarding permission, write to Bellwether Media, Inc., Attention: Permissions Department, 5357 Penn Avenue South, Minneapolis, MN 55419.

Library of Congress Cataloging-in-Publication Data

Names: Borgert-Spaniol, Megan, 1989- author.
Title: Northern Cardinals / by Megan Borgert-Spaniol.
Description: Minneapolis, MN : Bellwether Media, Inc., [2018] | Series:
   Blastoff! Readers: North American Animals | Audience: Age 5-8. | Audience:
   K to grade 3. | Includes bibliographical references and index.
Identifiers: LCCN 2016052735 (print) | LCCN 2017009469 (ebook) | ISBN
   9781626176409 (hardcover : alk. paper) | ISBN 9781681033709 (ebook)
Subjects: LCSH: Northern cardinal–Juvenile literature.
Classification: LCC QL696.P2438 B67 2018 (print) | LCC QL696.P2438 (ebook) |
   DDC 598.8/83–dc23
LC record available at https://lccn.loc.gov/2016052735

Editor: Nathan Sommer   Designer: Josh Brink

Printed in the United States of America, North Mankato, MN.

Table of Contents

What Are Northern Cardinals?

Northern cardinals are colorful birds that love to sing.

N
W E
S

Extinct

Extinct in the Wild

Critically Endangered

Endangered

Vulnerable

Near Threatened

Least Concern

northern cardinal range = ☐

conservation status: least concern

The birds are found in Canada, the United States, and **Central America**. They live as far south as Guatemala!

Northern cardinals live in a lot of different **habitats**. Many make their homes in woodlands or **swamps**. Others can be found in deserts.

They are also spotted near bird feeders in backyards and city gardens.

Northern cardinals mainly eat seeds and fruit. But these **omnivores** also snack on insects and spiders.

On the Menu

dogwood
berries

blackberries

wild grapes

sunflower seeds

field crickets

caterpillars

The birds often stay in low bushes. They hop between branches to find food.

Wings, Tails, and Crests

These songbirds measure up to 9 inches (23 centimeters) long. Their **wingspan** is about 12 inches (30 centimeters).

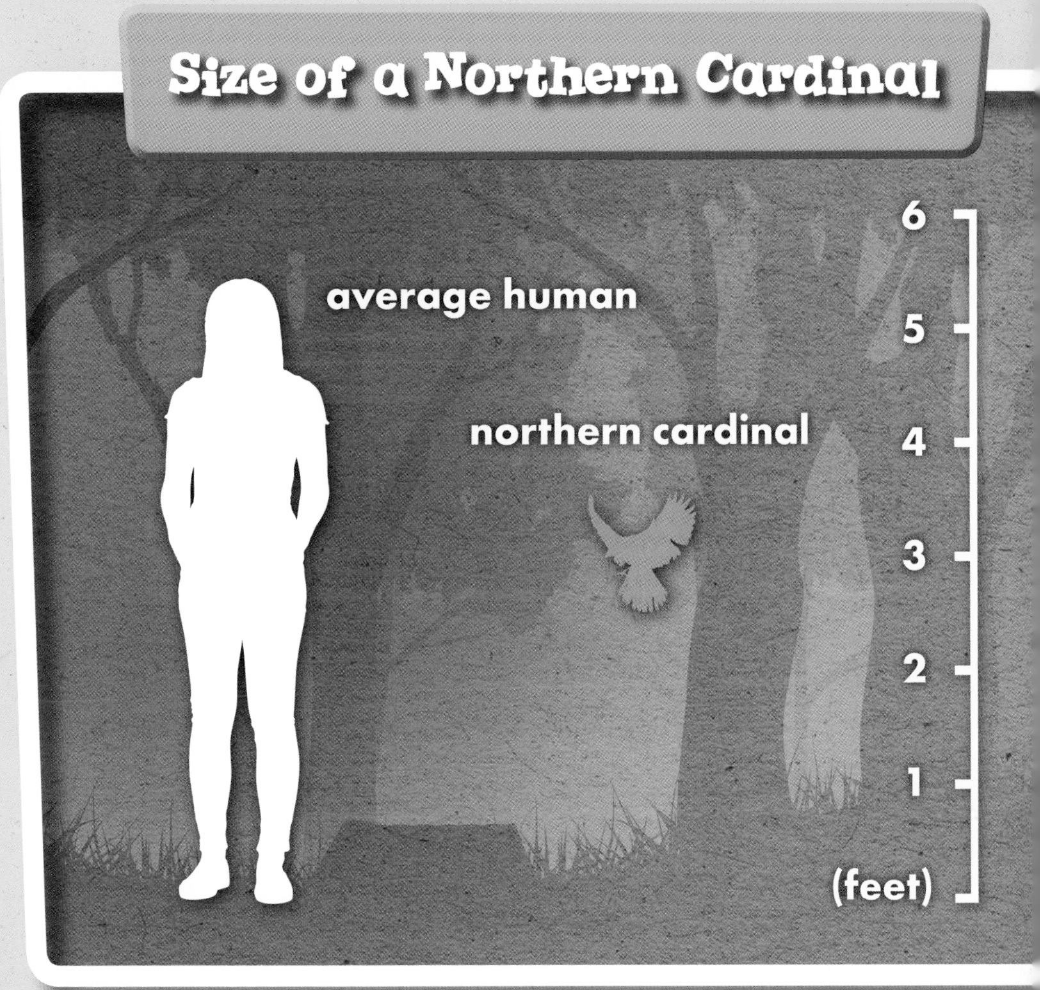

Size of a Northern Cardinal

average human

northern cardinal

6
5
4
3
2
1

(feet)

Their long tails point
straight down as the
birds rest on branches.

11

Identify a Northern Cardinal

crest feathers   black mask   orange bill

Northern cardinals have orange bills, black masks, and tall **crests**.

male

female

Males are known for their bright red color. Females are light brown with red wings, tails, and crests.

Nesting

Northern cardinals build nests each spring. The birds gather twigs, grasses, and leaves. Then, females bend them into a cup-shaped nest.

They tuck the nest between the branches of a shrub or small tree.

Females lay eggs in the nest. They sit on the eggs to keep them warm.

Males bring the females
food during this time. They
also fight other males that
come near the nest.

Cardinal Chicks

After about two weeks, **chicks** hatch. They are covered in soft, gray feathers. Mothers and their babies blend in with the nest. This keeps them hidden from **predators** like hungry snakes and hawks.

Baby Facts

Name for babies:	chicks
Number of eggs laid:	2 to 5 eggs
Time spent inside egg:	11 to 13 days
Time spent with parents:	1 to 2 months

Parents bring insects for their babies to eat.

After one to two weeks, the chicks spread their wings. They are ready to fly!

Glossary

Central America—the narrow, southern part of North America

chicks—baby northern cardinals

crests—bunches of hair on top of northern cardinals' heads

habitats—lands with certain types of plants, animals, and weather

omnivores—animals that eat both plants and animals

predators—animals that hunt other animals for food

swamps—wetlands filled with trees and other woody plants

wingspan—the distance between the tip of one wing to the tip of the other

To Learn More

AT THE LIBRARY
Alderfer, Jonathan K. *National Geographic Kids Bird Guide of North America: The Best Birding Book for Kids from National Geographic's Bird Experts.* Washington, D.C.: National Geographic, 2013.

Amstutz, Lisa J. *Cardinals*. North Mankato, Minn.: Capstone Press, 2016.

Mara, Wil. *Cardinals*. New York, N.Y.: Cavendish Square, 2015.

ON THE WEB
Learning more about northern cardinals is as easy as 1, 2, 3.

1. Go to www.factsurfer.com.

2. Enter "northern cardinals" into the search box.

3. Click the "Surf" button and you will see a list of related web sites.

With factsurfer.com, finding more information is just a click away.

Index

The images in this book are reproduced through the courtesy of: Bonnie Taylor Barry, front cover, p. 13; KellyNelson, p. 4; Rolf Nussbaumer Photography/ Alamy, p. 6; Drew Horne, p. 7; Martha Marks, p. 8; Oleg Mayorov, p. 9 (top left); Valentina Razumova, p. 9 (top right); zetat, p. 9 (center left); bergamont, p. 9 (center right); 2happy, p. 9 (bottom left); HelloRF Zcool, p. 9 (bottom right); Phil Lowe, p. 10; Steve Byland, p. 12 (top left, top center, top right); JLFCapture, p. 14; jimd_stock, p. 15; Gay Bumgarner/ Alamy, p. 16; William Leaman/ Alamy, p. 17; nikitsin.smugmug.com, p. 18; rck_953, p. 19; SWCargill, p. 20; All Canada Photos/ Alamy, p. 21.